CREATING A RIPPLE:

Serving Millions with
Mercy & Compassion
through Hospitality

LaToya Sharee

CREATING A RIPPLE JOURNAL

(FREE Resource: $49 Value)

Before you dive in the ocean and begin learning how to create ripples, open your computer or smart phone and **go to www.creatingaripple.com, enter your name and email address and follow the simple instructions to maximize the ripples you are going to create in every area of your life.**

This can be done easily – all you have to do is get this journal that walks you through your day so you are able to be intentional and conscience of the steps you are taking.

The resource link will come directly to your email and you will be able to download instantly – just open your email and enjoy!

Again, **go to www.creatingaripple.com, enter your name and email address and follow the simple instructions to maximize the ripples you are going to create in every area of your life NOW!**

The Guide to Serving Millions with
MERCY & COMPASSION
through Hospitality

LATOYA SHAREE
Atlanta, Georgia

Unless otherwise indicated, scripture quotations are from the Holy Bible, New International Version, Modern English Version and Amplified Version

All the stories related in this book are true, but most of the names have been changed to protect the privacy of the person mentioned.

Creating a Ripple: The Guide to Serving Millions with Mercy and Compassion through Hospitality

Copyright© 2016 by LaToya Sharee
Published in the United States by VP Group

ISBN - 0692768726

All rights reserved. No portion of this book may be reproduced, stored in a retrieval system or transmitted in any form or by any means – electronic, mechanical, photocopy, recording or other – except for brief quotations in printed reviews, without the prior written authorization of the author.

Printed in the United States of America

Edited by Dee Crawford

First Edition

"I'm not that smart." was a statement I often made when I did things that were outside of my comfort zone. These things could be successful, thoughts that were genius or the various "Ah Ha!" moments throughout my day that were so unlike me. After writing this book, I comfortably and confidently know whole-heartedly that statement isn't true because You are within me. You created me in Your likeness and image. I AM that Smart! I AM Wise! I AM Brilliant! You are the most amazing being and I love You so much. Lord, this book is dedicated to You. I would like to first honor and thank the Holy Spirit for giving me the ability, gift and talent to move forward and help others hone their gifts as well. Lord, I love You more than life itself and my appreciation goes beyond the most exquisite words that have been defined in the dictionary.

As the tears flow down my face I am so honored and grateful for this opportunity to be used by You. I pray that everyone that touches this book and reads this page is blessed. Cover them from the top of their heads to the soles of their feet. Meet all of their needs as they gain a personal and more intimate relationship with You.

Table of Contents

Foreward x

Introduction xi

Glossary xv

Chapter One 3
Let's Talk Hospitality!
What is hospitality?

Chapter Two 15
Going beyond the Call of Duty:
Exceeding Expectations

Chapter Three 19
Providing hospitality everywhere!

Chapter Four 27
Benefits of showing hospitality

Chapter Five 31
Someone's Always Watching and Listening

Chapter Six 39
Serving with your Heart
Do it on Purpose

Chapter Seven 43
Unity: It's a part of the process

Chapter Eight 47
Displaying Mercy & Compassion

Chapter Nine **51**
What Stops Your Hospitality?
Ways to Create a Ripple

Chapter Ten **55**
Is hospitality for you?

Wrap Up! **57**

As you read the words that jump off these pages I want you to know that I didn't just write this book, I lived it. There were so many distractions that came up and interrupted my life during the writing of this book as well as great influences. The stories and scenarios in this book are real life experiences. I challenge you to put yourself in the story if you can. Soften your heart and open your ears as well as your eyes. Change is here and waiting for you.

Foreward

LATOYA SHAREE IS an expert and God's gift to the body of Christ concerning Hospitality. In this book, she shares valuable nuggets on how to present the best for your business or ministry concerning Hospitality.

Dr. Jamie Pleasant; Ph.D.
Senior Pastor, New Zion Chrisitan Church
www.newzionchristianchurch.org
August 2016

Introduction

HAVE YOU EVER walked into a store and the sales associate looked into your eyes and walked past you without saying a word? Well, have you??? How did that experience make you feel? Did you stay and shop in that store or did you leave immediately and complain about how rude the experience was? I've been in that same situation plenty of times and I didn't feel appreciated even though I had just entered their store. I became highly upset because I did not feel welcome in their establishment to spend my hard earned money. I took action and asked to speak to management. I let them know exactly how I felt and gave them some suggestions so that other people that entered their establishment wouldn't feel the same way I did.

Some people don't understand that being hospitable is extremely important outside the industry of hospitality. The capacity for hospitality is actually being developed as we grow in the womb and it is nurtured at home with family and friends. It is deeper than we know it to be. Teaching and raising our children the right way and being an example to those that are not biologically ours is extremely important in this life. We have the position to change the world by creating ripples. We must learn to communicate effectively while being transparent and unashamed of our weaknesses. We should be interested in the story of those that are around us and as a result, selfishness will take a back seat.

With everything that is going on in this world of ours such as death and murder between mother and child or police and citizens, spiking crime rates, homelessness, human neglect, school shootings, racism, suicide; the list goes on, it's time for a change and the time is NOW. Believe it or not, it starts with YOU. So my question is, **"Are you ready?"**

My Life Changing Moment

INITIALLY, MY REASONS for writing this book were very simple but after lots of researching and me having to go back to the original definition of the word Hospitality. I found that I needed to take more time and go back to the basics and really dig deep to find out more. I realized that I didn't know as much as I thought I did. In this book, you will learn how to create ripples of love in every aspect of your life. We will go deeper than learning how to make your holiday parties better. We will learn how to build great relationships with strangers, the ones you love and cherish, to seeing a homeless person in a different way. This book is going to make you think and hopefully change the way you look at your life, others and the world as a whole.

From janitorial workers, restaurant servers, stay at home mom/dads, police officers to CEOs of multi-billion dollar corporations, this book is for everyone. Read with an open heart and mind and think of the many ways you can incorporate and start creating ripples in your everyday life. Let's do this by creating ripples and practicing hospitality.

Creating a ripple is the spiritual way to pay it forward. I am excited for you and the change you are about to experience. Take a moment to think and examine your life because in just a few short days and weeks it is going to change drastically.

Glossary

Words you will need to familiarize yourself with as you go through this book.

Assist: *(verb)* To help; to aid; to succor; to give support to in undertaking or effort, or in time of distress.

Benefit: *(noun)* An act of kindness; a favor conferred (verb transitive) to do good; to advantage; to advance in health or prosperity (verb intransitive) to gain advantage; to make improvements.

Compassion: *(noun)* A suffering with on another; painful sympathy; at least some portion of love generally attends the pain or regret, or is excited by it (verb) to pity.

Customer Service: *(verb)* The assistance and advice provided by a company to those people who buy or use its products or services.

Entertain: *(verb)* To treat with conversation; to amuse or instruct by discourse; properly, to engage the attention and retain the company of one, by agreeable conversation, discourse or argument.

Expectation: *(noun)* The act of expecting or looking forward to a future event with at least some reason to believe the event will happen.

Friend: *(noun)* One who is attached to another by affection; one who entertains for another sentiments of esteem, respect and affection, which lead him to desire his company, and to seek to promote his happiness and prosperity; opposed to foe or enemy.

Generous: *(adjective)* strong; full of spirit; overflowing; abundant, courageous; free to give; liberal; munificent.

Give: *(verb)* to have; to turn over the possession or control of to someone without cost or exchange; a gift; to hand or pass over into trust or keeping of someone.

Heart: *(noun)* the seat of the affections and passions, as of love, joy, grief, enmity, courage, pleasure etc: to go exceedingly and abundantly above what is required.

Help: *(verb)* to aid; to assist; to lend strength or means towards effecting a purpose; to help one to pay his debts; to relieve; to cure; to remedy; to change for the better.

Hospitality: *(noun)* the act or practice of receiving and entertaining strangers or guests without reward, or with kind and generous liberality.

Host: *(noun)* one who entertains another at his own house, without reward.

Humble: *(adverb)* to be made low, abased, rendered meek and submissive; penitent.

Integrity: *(noun)* wholeness; entireness; unbroken state; purity; genuine, unadulterated, unimpaired state.

Mercy: *(noun)* pity; compassion manifested toward a person in distress; clemency and bounty.

Passion: *(noun)* the impression or effect of an external agent upon a body; that which is suffered or received; suffering; emphatically, the last suffering of the Savior.

Patience: *(noun)* a calm temper with bears evils without murmuring or discontent; the act or quality of waiting long for justice or expected good without discontent.

Power: *(noun)* force; strength; energy.

Practice: *(noun)* repeated exercise in or performance of an activity or skill so as to acquire or maintain proficiency in it.

Praise: *(verb)* to commend; to applaud; to express approbation of a personal worth or action; to do honor to; to display the excellence of.

Pursue: *(verb)* to follow, to go or proceed after or in a like direction; to seek; to use measures to obtain.

Sacrifice: *(verb)* to offer to God in homage or worship; to destroy, surrender or suffer to be lost for the sake of obtaining something; to devote with loss.

Serve: *(verb)* to act as the minister of; to perform official duties to; to attend at command; to wait on; to work for.

Service: *(noun)* public worship or office of devotion; that which God requires of man; worship; obedience.

Stranger: *(noun)* one who belongs to another country, town, city; one unknown; one unacquainted; a guest; a visitor.

Synergy: *(noun)* combined or cooperative action, joint work, to work together.

Togetherness: *(noun)* the state of being close to another person or other people, a feeling of closeness or affection from being united with other people.

Unity: *(noun)* a state of being one; oneness; concord; agreement; uniformity.

Value: *(noun)* ones worth; price; high rate; importance (verb) to take an account of; to reckon.

Welcome: *(adjective)* received with gladness; grateful; pleasing; free to have or enjoy gratuitously (noun) salutation of a new comer; kind reception of a guest.

Wisdom: *(noun)* the right use or exercise of knowledge; gained by experience; quickness of intellect; readiness of apprehension.

Chapter One

Let's Talk Hospitality!

Do not be conformed to this world, but be transformed by the renewing of your mind, that you may prove what is the good and acceptable and perfect will of God.

– Romans 12:2 (MEV)

HAVE YOU EVER thought about and compared the words hospitality and customer service? In all honesty, customer service is just a watered down phrase that took the place of hospitality as the world started taking church out of everything. As individuals, it is our responsibility to bridge the gap between the church and state and start incorporating hospitality in our everyday walk and language- where it should have been the entire time.

WHAT IS HOSPITALITY?

Let's look at the definitions…

The original Greek word for hospitality in the Bible is philoxenia (φιλοξενία). Below you will see this word can be broken down into two parts.

1. *philo* - meaning love
2. *xenia* - meaning strangers (you may think of xenophobia, as in the fear of strangers)

The biblical meaning of hospitality is the love of strangers.

Now that we see the definition of the word, I would like us to go a little further with breaking down the definitions of each word then putting it all back together.

Love: Most people would say the meaning of love is very complex but in all actuality we are the ones that make it so hard and complicated. Love is an action that needs to be shown multiple times throughout the day to everyone we come in contact with.

Every Christian refers to 1 Corinthians 13:4-8 to define love. After reading these verses, you will be able to get a full and deeper understanding of what love is and why we should love. Before you skip down to verses 4-8 let's start at verses 1-3.

1 Corinthians 13:1 Oh wait…let's look at the verse before. 1 Corinthians 12:31 Backdrop: The first half of Chapter 12 talks in-depth about your Spiritual Gifts and the second part explains how we are one body with

many parts. At the end of Chapter 12 God, through Paul, so eloquently says ³¹·***But eagerly desire the greater gifts. And now I will show you the most excellent way.***

How awesome is that? God loves us so much that he decided to show us how to exercise our spiritual gifts through love. Read that verse again and meditate on it for a couple of minutes before moving forward.

What are your thoughts about those verses?

_____
_____
_____

1 Corinthians 13:1-8
"If I speaking the tongues of men and of angels, but have not love, I am only a resounding gong or a clanging symbol. ²If I have the gift of prophecy and can fathom all mysteries and all knowledge, and if I have a faith that call move mountains, but have not love, I am nothing. ³If I give all I possess to the poor and surrender my body to the flames, but have not loved, I gain nothing. ⁴Love is patient, love is kind. It does not envy, it does not boast, it is not proud.

⁵It is not rude, it is not self-seeking, it is not easily angered, it keeps no record of wrongs. ⁶Love does not delight in evil but rejoices with the truth. ⁷It always protects, always trusts, always hopes, always perseveres. ⁸Love never fails. But where there are prophecies, they

will cease; where there are tongues, they will be stilled; where there is knowledge, it will pass away."

Take a moment to meditate on those scriptures before moving forward. Do you see why love is important? It is vital to our lives because it allows us to grow not only our relationship with others but our relationship with God.

Since we are always changing and growing, did you realize we can be strangers to each other whether we have been around someone your whole life or not? To gain a deeper understanding, let's break down the types of love then we will go into the meaning of the word stranger.

TYPES OF LOVE

Phileo: affectionate and warm, how you feel about someone, platonic, friendship

Eros: lover, passionate intense love, romantic feelings for someone. sexual feelings between a man and a woman.

Agape: unconditional, this type of love goes beyond the surface and is accepted no matter how many flaws or imperfections the person has. This is the most difficult love to display. This is the "under any and all circumstances" love.

Now you can go back to 1 Corinthians 13:4 and really get the true meaning of love…its agape. I call it "that no matter what love".

Now, let's take a look at the meaning of the word stranger.

Stranger: A newcomer, a visitor, an outsider, a person not known or familiar to one.

Can you see how you are a stranger to not only others but to yourself? Every time you go through something you learn something new about yourself and others. As we move back into the realm of hospitality we must understand that it is not just about how great your house smells around the holidays or inviting your friends and family over to enjoy meals.

Hospitality started before we were born. The perfect example was from the one who created us. God practiced hospitality with us first.

The ultimate level of hospitality is shown in John 3:16.

"*For God so love the world that he gave his one and only Son that whoever believes in him shall not perish but have eternal (everlasting) life. For God did not send his Son into the world to condemn the world, but to save the world through him.*" That is true hospitality. This is one of many scriptures that God not only shows us how to practice hospitality but leads by example, the perfect example.

All throughout the Holy Bible you will see specific scriptures stating how we all are aliens and strangers of this world which means that our true home was with God the Father in Heaven.

Leviticus 19:33-34 states,

"When an alien lives with you in your land, do not mistreat him. ³⁴The alien living with you must be treated as one of your native-born. Love him as yourself, for you were aliens in Egypt. I am the Lord your God."

Let's take a moment to meditate on Leviticus 19:33-34. It took me a while to really understand what God was showing me about strangers and loving them no matter who they were or what place they were in their life.

An old friend once told me that you have to meet people where they are. After continuing to converse with them I understood more of them and where they were coming from. I then began to see them for who they were not who I wanted them to be.

Everyone is a stranger whether you know them or not. You should never say you know the people you are around inside and out. Yes, you can learn them but you will never KNOW them. Because of how we were created, learned behaviors, rejections, and life happening, we can change at the drop of a dime. What do people always say? I thought I knew him/her? Or didn't think he/she would ever do that.

Going a little deeper, you think you really know yourself but you don't. God is the only one that knows everything about us. And there are times where we even shock God in the things we do.

HOW MANY STRANGERS DO YOU KNOW NOW?

So, what usually comes to mind when you think of hospitality? Let's take a moment to see what the world thinks of hospitality.
- Making sure your house is clean before friends and family come over for fun and fellowship.
- The feeling you have when your life is in order and everything is going "peachy keen".
- Smiling in people's face to get what you want at a specific moment in time.
- Being nice to your grandparents just because they are old and you will receive an inheritance when they cross over.
- Being passive and agreeing with a statement that goes against your morals just to allow the situation to pass.

Isn't it odd that the world thinks of those statements as hospitality? It seems more like customer service wouldn't you think?

The difference between customer service and hospitality is providing customer service is only shown for a moment but hospitality lasts a lifetime. Hospitality is about cultivating relationships. Think about the impact and impression you are leaving on others. Would you rather give them customer service or provide hospitality?

Read the three scenarios below and choose the best scenario that would describe "hospitality" as defined here.

1. Your spouse, significant other or really good friend begins to take the food out of the oven while you finish setting the dining room table with beautiful new plate sets you just purchased. You suddenly hear the doorbell ring. Before hurrying to the door, you stop in the foyer to turn down the music you had playing in the background as you cleaned the house. Opening the door together, you greet your guests with a warm smile and greeting. "Hey, Welcome to our home, come on in. How have you been?" Your guests smile as they enter your home flaring their nostrils at the wonderful smelling food cooking in the kitchen, looking around as they walked through the living room admiring the beautiful holiday decorations.
2. After turning in an extensive project proposal and being awake for over 52 hours, you lay down to rest and begin to doze off. Thirty-two minutes after nestling in your warm

bed you hear a hard knock at the door. You wake up startled and begin wondering who it could be because you are not expecting anyone. You begin wiping the drool from your mouth as you get up to open the door. There is a husband and wife at the door asking if they could have something to eat. They've explained that they have been staying in their rental car in the cold for two days after being evicted out of their home and they don't have any money. You wipe the crust from your eye and invite them in. After asking them to sit down at your kitchen table you remembered the feast you cooked for yourself the day before and start to warm it up for them. You put fresh crescent rolls in the oven and poured them a glass of water. You also offer them a glass of your unopened 2008 Spottswoode Cabernet Sauvignon that you purchased from California when you were there on business.

3. As you walk into your favorite restaurant you are greeted with smile and verbal greetings as they seat you in a section with a beautiful view of the waterfall on the pond. You begin to look at the menu and decide what you are going to eat.

Which scenario describes true hospitality?
_____
_____
_____

If you said all of the statements show hospitality you would be correct. However, go back and look closely. All of the scenarios show different levels of hospitality. Which level of hospitality should we strive to provide daily if we get the opportunity? Scenario #2 is the correct answer. Practicing true hospitality is not always planned and in scenario #2, this instance would be the best display of hospitality. The space to practice hospitality will come when you decide to release or sacrifice something that is important to you. Hospitality is not always comfortable.

The cliché: Treat others like you want to be treated is very true when it comes to hospitality. I would like to take it a little bit further and say, treat others BETTER than you want to be treated.

When you start to practice this, you will begin to understand why you are lacking in some areas of your life, if not all.

Before I realized this truth, I thought the same thing. Treating others like I wanted to be treated is great but if you treat them better, yours and their experience would be over the top! Don't just be average, go ahead and take that extra step and exceed expectations. Yes, it is a little more work to do but you will be rewarded for it in time.

In the upcoming chapters, we will discuss the benefits of practicing hospitality.

Most people think that hospitality is just practiced in the industry that involves waiters, waitresses; or servants that clean up after you when leaving a hotel or vacation location and that is not true. As you start to look deeper into the true meaning of the word hospitality you will understand that it is a <u>human experience</u> and it started in the biblical days. Hospitality is something that everyone should take advantage of now.

True Hospitality is born in your inner most being (soul), transferred to your heart, displayed through your hands, then heard from your mouth.

HOW DO I CREATE A RIPPLE?

The definition of a ripple is a small wave or series of waves on the surface of water, especially as caused by an object dropping into it or a slight breeze; a particular feeling or effect that spreads through or to someone or something.

Think of creating a ripple in practical terms. You hear your favorite lyricist or musician playing the saxophone or piano, bass or drums. Or the awesome man of God that God has placed in your life to speak over you at your church. The amazing feeling you feel when you close your eyes and listen to them is the same feeling that everyone you come into contact with should feel when you serve them with everything you have inside of you.

Create A Ripple of Love
Create A Ripple of Unity
Create A Ripple of Peace
Create A Ripple of Service

What ripples will you create?

There is always an opportunity to practice hospitality. Start creating yours today.

As you continue to read, I challenge you to open up more than you have ever done before; not just to God but to others as well.

John 15:12-15

My command is this: Love each other as I have loved you. 13 Greater love has no one than this, that he lay down his life for his friends. 14 You are my friends if you do what I command. 15 I no longer call you servants, because a servant does not know his master's business. Instead, I have called you friends, for everything that I learned from my Father I have made known to you.

Chapter Two

Going beyond the Call of Duty & Exceeding Expectations

Whatever you do, work at it with all your heart, as working for the Lord, not for human masters, since you know that you will receive an inheritance from the Lord as a reward. It is the Lord Christ you are serving.
– Colossians 3:23

AS YOU BEGIN to practice hospitality you shouldn't just do the bare minimum, you should go big or go home. We all want to be seen doing something great at some point of our life so why not allow that dream to come true all the time. It shouldn't matter if someone else is looking. When it comes to hospitality, the more you start doing for others the more relaxed and open you will feel. Practicing hospitality will allow you to get to know the real you as you do for others. If you don't believe me, just try to put others needs before your own for 15 minutes a day and see if it doesn't benefit you and change your life. You are going to have to be selfless when practicing hospitality.

In Chapter 1, we went over the meaning of the word hospitality, what the world thinks about it and how people work in and around it.

Now let's talk about how we can go beyond the call of duty and exceed the expectations of others in and outside the industry of hospitality.

You will be tested and placed in different situations that will allow you to take advantage of the skills you possess.

Above all love each other deeply, because love covers a multitude of sins. ⁹ Offer hospitality to one another without grumbling. 1 Peter 4:8-9

This scripture definitely takes it to the next level. You are not able to talk about hospitality without talking about love. Have you ever heard of the phrase "southern hospitality"? Does that mean you can't provide hospitality in the northern, western and eastern states or any were else in the world? Absolutely not! Southern Hospitality is a phrase used in the English language to describe the residents living in the Southern United States below the Mason Dixon line and their common and well-known disposition to family and strangers.

The phrase was coined in the early 1800's and it was described as sweet, welcoming, willingness to serve, being gracious and displaying kindness. Can you provide southern hospitality in the northern states? Yes, you definitely can.

Remember, hospitality means the love of strangers. Hospitality starts in the spirit and then manifests in the flesh. Practice hospitality in your homes, community and church. We have to be intentional and remember that the focus is to love strangers.

"The most important one," and answered Jesus, "is this: Hear, O Israel the Lord our God, the Lord is one. Love the Lord your God with all your heart and with all your soul and with all your mind and with all your strength. 31 The second is this: 'Love your neighbor as yourself.' There is no commandment greater than these." Mark 12:29-31

Chapter Three

Providing hospitality everywhere!

²Do not neglect to show hospitality to strangers, for by this some have entertained angels without knowing it.

– Hebrew 13:2

I REMEMBER THINKING years ago that showing hospitality everywhere could never be done. When I started working in the hospitality industry I found out it was something that had to actually be done daily. I became a lot more conscience of the action of hospitality. I found myself turning into "that person," the person that always looked for ways to compliment and/or give to others. I began to see and feel the benefits of practicing hospitality. I was creating ripples of love everywhere I placed my feet and my life started getting better. No one was able to stop me and believe me they tried. Everyone started to love being around me. As the weeks, months and years passed they wanted to know what I was doing that made me smile every time they came into contact with me.

I told them that it was the love in my heart, how I felt and how making people feel good made *me* happy.

In the beginning, some people didn't believe me but as they started paying attention to everything I did, they began to see it for themselves. It became contagious and explosive!

Love is mentioned over 400 times in the Holy Bible depending on the version you are reading. As we discussed earlier, the number one scripture that everyone uses to define and describe love but the least applied is from 1 Corinthians 13:4-8 and it reads

[4]Love is patient, love is kind. It does not envy, it does not boast, it is not proud. [5] It is not rude, it is not self-seeking, it is not easily angered, it keeps no record of wrongs. [6]Love does not delight in evil but rejoices with the truth. [7]It always protects, always trusts, always hopes, always perseveres. [8]Love never fails. But where there are prophecies, they will cease; where there are tongues, they will be stilled; where there is knowledge, it will pass away.

As you read over those verses again, ask yourself if this is the type of love you are practicing and displaying in your life everyday…not just once or twice a week or when it benefits you, but every single day. Are you creating a ripple of love everywhere you go and with every one you come into contact with? Practicing hospitality is not going to be easy but it is simple.

Every time I read those verses I have to check myself. None of us are perfect but we are being perfected in Christ daily.

Practice doesn't make perfect, it makes permanent. If you miss a day of showing love to others, just show more the next day. God will always provide an opportunity for you to show love.

You can be hospitable any and everywhere. No matter how hard you try, you will never be able to run away from providing hospitality in some way.

Whether you are with your spouse/significant other, parents, at church or work and even by yourself, there will always be an opportunity to provide or practice it. If you have to, refer back to Chapter 1 and look at the definition again.

LET'S TALK HOSPITALITY!!!

Below, are some examples of hospitality being practiced in common areas of our life. Feel free to add your own examples that you can reference. These are simple things that we take for granted or tasks that we don't think are important.

HOME

- Saying good morning and good night when we are in the presence of others
- Think before you speak to your kids, parents and spouse/significant other
- Take the time to help your kids with their homework and other things
- Smiling and laughing with your family
- Help cook breakfast, lunch and/or dinner
- _____
- _____

WORK/BUSINESS

- Speaking to everyone you interact with on your way to the office and in your office
- Help others become as efficient as you
- Train others to do your job
- Saying Please and Thank you
- Exceed your clients/customers expectations
- Conduct business the correct way
- Showing respect at all times
- Being honest with yourself and others
- Share special techniques for others to succeed
- _____
- _____

CHURCH

- Speaking and hugging everyone you see
- Pray for someone other than yourself
- Showing respect
- Pray for the leaders of your church everyday
- Tithe at least 10% from every paycheck
- Encourage and compliment others
- Serving the Pastors and Ministers
- Assist when and where there is a need
- Be patient with others
- Get to know someone new
- Listen and open up to others about your life
- _____
- _____

SCHOOL

- Smiling and speaking to others
- Helping others with homework
- Giving students school tours
- Showing respect
- Assisting the teachers
- Being an example to others
- Listen to others
- _____
- _____

Providing hospitality everywhere!

FAMILY FUNCTIONS

- Fixing food plates for others
- Showing respect
- Serving others first
- Listen to others
- _____
- _____

WHILE SHOPPING

- Speaking to everyone that passes you
- Pay for someone's food/items
- Showing respect
- Let someone skip you in line
- Speak to others you pass
- Make eye contact when you speak
- _____
- _____

HOSPITALS

- Speak to everyone you make eye contact with
- Visit people
- Show respect
- Pray for the sick
- Create a card or take flowers
- _____
- _____

RESTAURANTS

- Be patient with your server
- Show others respect in restaurant
- Tip your server 20%, 22% 25%+
- Leave your phone in the car or at home
- _____
- _____

HOTELS

- Tip the housekeeper
- Speak to the staff at the front desk
- Be nice and intentional
- _____
- _____

EVERYWHERE

- Consider the feelings of others when you interact with them throughout the day
- Show respect
- Say please and thank you
- Think before you speak
- Consider others feelings
- _____
- _____

Chapter Four

Benefits of showing hospitality

Share with God's people who are in need. Practice Hospitality – Romans 12:13

THERE ARE MANY benefits that come with practicing hospitality. Peace, joy, gaining a sense of accomplishment and a boost in your self esteem.

PHYSICAL HEALTH

Your attitude and countenance will change. You will begin to smile more. Your body will begin to heal from the inside out. You will carry patience everywhere you go. You will become beautiful to everyone you come in contact with but most importantly to yourself.

EMOTIONAL HEALTH

You will become open and aware of the needs of others. Practicing hospitality will boost your self esteem. Joy will begin to run through your body like a lightning bolt. It takes away depression. You will begin to feel a sense of worthiness.

MENTAL HEALTH

Your mind will become clear. God will begin to give you discernment and show you who to assist, help and pray for. You will begin understand how to carry and distribute peace. You will be aware of your thoughts and be able to dismiss anything that doesn't line up with the will of God. Your focus will become stronger than ever.

SPIRITUAL HEALTH

You will become more like Christ. You will begin to live and depend on Him through each experience. You will realize that God is in control of every situation you face. Your prayer life will increase. And because you will decide to put others before you (as God leads) and take care of God's business, He will make sure you are taken care of in every area of your life. Your faith will become unbreakable.

As you continue to practice hospitality, God will begin to make Himself known to you more and more.

Your visions and dreams will become vivid and full of color. You will begin to open your heart and receive your God given purpose.

This may look like it's a lot and may even seem overwhelming. It won't happen all at once, but you will see as well as feel the difference in yourself as you continue to create ripples of love. Practicing hospitality should never stop. It's a lifestyle not a destination!

ACTIVITY #1

Start a written and/or video journal and keep up with what you've done, how you've shared and the words you've spoken. It will be tough in the beginning but I believe in you and you know that you will be consistent. Writing will begin to become a part of your everyday life. The Creating a Ripple Journal explains how writing in a journal inproves your quality of life.

To download your <u>Creating a Ripple Journal</u> visit, www.creatingaripple.com/resources and get it for FREE!

Chapter Five

Someone's Always Watching & Listening

"Above all else, guard your heart, for everything you do flows from it. ²⁴Keep your mouth free of perversity; keep corrupt talk far from your lips."

– Proverbs 4:23-24 (NIV)

WE LIVE IN a world of watchful eyes and open ears. No matter where you are someone is always watching you and listening to you. This is not just the case with our children. As we place ourselves in different positions and situations throughout our life, we are under surveillance. It could be while we are talking on the phone, shopping and/or cooking, you are never alone. As we enter into this chapter we will discover the importance of using our words and how they affect others as well as yourself.

A few years back, I was sitting in a training class and the seasoned employees of the company were sitting behind me talking about and judging everyone that introduced themselves to the rest of the team members. Immediately my spirit began to grieve for them and I started praying that God would keep me focused and attentive to the training. Thinking they were whispering they continued to mumble and laugh to each other. They called specific people idiots, loudly saying how they didn't like them and being extremely rude. After a couple of hours our trainer asked us to go on break. As I got up from my seat and headed out the door for lunch, one of my team members pulled me aside and asked me if I could pray with her because her heart was heavy. She began to explain to me that she heard the negative comments the seasoned team members were saying and she wasn't able to focus because it didn't sit right with her. This was a wow moment for me because the new team member was sitting in front of me so I didn't think she heard them.

Luke 6:45 says,

"A good man (woman) brings good things out of the good stored up in his (her) heart, and an evil man (woman) brings evil things out of the evil stored up in his heart. For the mouth speaks what the heart is full of."

Watch where you are, the thoughts you have and what you say. You need to be aware and know that there is someone always listening regardless if you see them or not.

Did you know incidents like this happen often throughout the day and we say or do nothing about it? Be mindful about what comes out of your mouth even when you are talking to yourself. It starts with a thought. As soon as your words come out of your mouth there is no way to put them back in. At that moment your character, respect and integrity may be compromised.

After hearing my soon to be co-workers talk about everyone in that manner it made me not want to work for the company anymore. It also made me realize that people like that need to experience more ripples of love in their personal life.

I hung in there to see if it was going to change but my number one concern and mission was to see if I could change the environment. I knew walking into work each day wouldn't be easy but I made it a priority to lead by example and show them lots of love through words to everyone. I started by taking a couple of the ladies out to lunch so I could get to know their true personalities away from the other individuals. They had great personalities, top notch industry skills and were hard working women. I really couldn't understand why they talked about the others like they did. A few months later, one ended up quitting because she wasn't happy nor fulfilled. Words can alter your vision.

If you are ever in that situation or a similar one, do

what's best for you. Go back and look at some of the suggested ways to create ripples of love that were stated in the previous chapters of this book and apply them.

One of the most important tasks that will come from creating ripples of love is that your prayer life will increase. In most cases if you are not able to physically change the situation you will definitely be able to change your spiritual outlook about the situation. It's all through prayer. Pray that God changes how you see people and ask God to give them a heart of service.

Whether you are in a position of influence or not you have to be mindful that you are going to always be the center for the simple reason that God set you apart. With the favor that God has given you, you will be watched and studied like a subject in school.

We underestimate the power we hold. The tongue is a small member of our body and holds more than your hands. The tongue is a weapon that could be a spoon to scoop someone up that has had a horrible day or it could be used as a knife to cut someone's life in half. Your tongue is also like a loaded gun! Once we understand that we are responsible for not just us but for other people, you will begin to use your tongue correctly. Be hospitable with your words.

Using peaceful and kind words will definitely change your life. Here are some words you can incorporate in your daily vocabulary. I call these words "My Extraordinary Love Word Bank". You have to put thought and effort into play when you decide to use these words and phrases. They won't come naturally especially if you don't hear them on a daily basis.

Delightful	Amazing
Awesome job	My pleasure
Thank you	I am proud of you
I appreciate you	You are welcome
Fantastic	I love you
Abundance	I AM Powerful
Extraordinary	Glorious
Magnificent	Miracle
Success	Beautiful
Wonderful	Enjoyable
Pleasant	Absolutely
Successful	Happy
Well	Motivated
I have power	Wealthy
Rich	Growth
Positive	I need help
Prosperous	Great job
I apologize	You can do it!
You inspire me	How are you doing?
Thankful	Inspire

ACTIVITY #2:

Create your own list. Add words or phrases that you would like to incorporate into your everyday language.

_____	_____
_____	_____
_____	_____
_____	_____
_____	_____
_____	_____
_____	_____
_____	_____

Don't worry if you are not able to fill all the blanks now. As you begin to practice hospitality you will receive words from others that you can write down.

ACTIVITY #3:

Let's take it a step further. Get 7 sticky notes and write one word on each piece of paper, then post them on your bathroom mirror. The purpose of this activity is to create a new image of yourself, boost your self esteem and build up others every day.

As you begin to use the words above remember that your voice tone, demeanor and attitude is just as powerful as the words are.

Imagine being on the phone with someone who is using these words but they sound like they are having a bad day or they are not smiling. It doesn't match. You may have to check yourself and get yourself together before picking up the phone.

Talk yourself into being happy even if you don't take well to the person on the other end of the line. It is not about you. You have to sacrifice your feelings and make that person feel like they are the last person on the earth and you need them. Make them feel wanted. Be intentional when it comes to using your words.

Chapter Six

Serving with Your Heart
Be Deliberate:
Do it on Purpose

*Do not withhold good from those who deserve it,
when it is in your power to act. Do not say to your
neighbor, "Come back later; I'll give it tomorrow" – when
you now have it with you.
– Proverbs 3:27*

SERVING GOES HAND and hand with practicing hospitality and creating positive ripples in your life. Something that we all want to hear when we stand before God is for Him to say, well done my good and faithful servant. In order for that to happen we must become servants. We were created to serve. Now, our lives have taken a front seat and we seem to have placed serving others at the bottom of the list. This is after we've finished every important thing we needed to do. I challenge you to rethink and rewrite/renumber your priority list.

Serving others is included in your purpose and if you are not aware of God's purpose for your life, just start serving others and you will begin to open up and find out.

When we talk about serving others I am not referring to working in a restaurant and taking orders. Now don't get me wrong, this is honestly how I found out the purpose that God has for me. It may not be the same for you. You are going to have to go outside of your comfort zone when it comes to serving others. It might not be your strong point but just like we talked about in the previous chapters, as you practice hospitality it will become a permanent and evident choice in your life.

As we set our life up for success, we have to be able to serve others. No matter what is going on, there will be a place and time for you to serve from your heart.

As stated in Chapter 1, most people think that hospitality is just an industry.

Make it a appoint to do something for or say something to someone every day. In the _16 Days of Hospitality Workbook_, you will find small suggestions and nuggets you can apply to your life without even thinking about it. Taking advantage of every opportunity will allow God to use you more than He has ever done before.

If you want to begin to create change in your life and the lives of others, get the workbook _16 Days of Hospitality_ by visiting, www.creatingaripple.com/resources and get it for FREE!

Chapter Seven

Unity and Togetherness... It's a Part of the Process

*How good and pleasant it is when
brothers live together in unity!*
– Psalm 133:1

HAVING UNITY AND togetherness is a huge part of practicing true hospitality and is a must when it comes to creating a ripple. It's all about relationship building. In Chapter 6, we talked a little about making sure we add "I need help" to our vocabulary. When the majority of people say this or when they hear that phrase it makes their skin crawl. There are two reasons why this might happen. (1) They asked for help before and either didn't receive the type of help they needed or received rejection after asking. (2) They've seen others get rejected and said "that will never happen to me" or they are just prideful perfectionists that don't want to acknowledge failures in their life.

Asking for help doesn't show weakness it actually shows strengths in you and trust in the person you are asking. There is no way that you are able to do anything by yourself. If you think you can, just take a moment to think about it and answer these questions.

- Who helped you enter the world?
- Who taught you how to tie your shoes?
- Who took you back and forth to school?
- Who fed you food?
- How did you gain income to survive?
- How did you pay for college?
- Who helped you start your business?
- Who assisted you with your homework?
- Who played with you in your childhood?
- Who taught you about the necessities of life?

Oh wait one more…Who woke you up this morning? Never take for granted the love that God shows you daily.

If Jesus could do nothing by himself, what makes you think you think we are any different?

John 5:19
"I tell you the truth, the Son can do nothing by

himself; he can do only what he sees his Father doing, because whatever the Father does the Son also does."

Whether you want to admit it or not, we all need help and if you still think you did everything on your own then think of how God has always made a way for you in every situation you have ever been in. Look at God's track record for your life and in the lives of others.

As you begin to experience togetherness, understand that it is one of the most amazing feelings a person could ever have. It is the sense of belonging or not feeling alone. As unity brings people together, togetherness keeps them together…One body, one mind, one spirit. The emotional feeling you gain is priceless. Togetherness is a family feeling. The true emotion of love.

With togetherness you will always have someone there for you, someone that understands you and someone who is willing to go that extra mile for you. Take a moment to think about your life. Are you creating ripples of unity and togetherness? If not, think of the things that are hindering you from creating those ripples. Be honest with yourself. The ultimate goal is for you to grow in love and create ripples in every area of your life.

Chapter Eight

Mercy & Compassion / Forgive

And be kind one to another, tenderhearted, forgiving one another, just as God in Christ also forgave you. – Ephesians: 4:32

I AM NOT able to talk about mercy and compassion without first tapping into forgiveness. Everyday God forgives you for everything you've said and done knowingly and unknowingly. He gives you an abundance of mercy and compassion.

As we strive to be like Christ and show His true character we must walk in forgiveness daily. Think of what it would be like if God didn't show you mercy and compassion daily. I couldn't even imagine what my day would be like without God's grace in my life. Back in Chapter 7 we talked about not doing anything on our own.

Take a moment to think about what would happen if God took His mercy and compassion away from us. The feeling would be unbearable. I personally don't think I could live through it. Every day that God allows us to take a breath is a demonstration of His mercy. We make mistakes on top of mistakes and God decides to show us compassion. If God didn't **LOVE** (show hospitality to) us like He does, He would have already destroyed the earth. Please understand that there is no running away from it. Hospitality is a vital part of our life whether we want to hear it or not. Don't think it is just an industry that you can work in. Take it personal and be intentional as you practice it. Create a Ripple of Forgiveness.

If it wasn't for God forgiving us every day we wouldn't be able to forgive others. Let's put it another way. If we don't forgive others God won't forgive us.

Matthew 6:15

"But if you don't forgive men for their sins, neither will your Father forgive your sins"

And Mark 11:26 says the same thing...

"But if you do not forgive, neither will your Father which is in heaven forgive your sins."

When it comes to forgiveness you must start with forgiving yourself which is really hard if you don't have an understanding of God's love. You have to take the necessary steps and understand that it is not going to get easy until you first bring everything to the surface, find the root cause, and talk about it. After that, you will be able to move forward.

When you forgive others you are actually doing yourself a favor. You are releasing yourself from bondage, as well as allowing God the opportunity to heal and bless you.

I think about the times I felt hurt, humiliated, embarrassed, or abandoned by someone I cared about or loved deeply or something I've done to someone else. During that time I put myself in a box not wanting to talk to, help or even look at the person or group of people. I didn't realize I was holding myself back and missing out on the peace and joy I could have had all along.

I held on to the offense for a while. That struggle lead to depression and me getting sick and losing confidence in what I knew God to be in my life.

Unforgiveness will attach to your body like a cancer; it is deeply rooted and the more you try to ignore it the more it will spread into other areas of your life and body. It is a disease. Unforgiveness will hurt your heart, allow you to become bitter and will block God's purpose from being visible in your life. Remember, love covers all.

Chapter Nine

What Stops Your Hospitality And Ways to Create a Ripple

Having a bad attitude
Anger issues
Being conceited
Low self esteem
Complaining
Fear
Deceitful
Unforgiveness
Manipulative
Lack of focus
Not applying wisdom
Showing favoritism

Over-thinking
Negative thoughts
Not loving yourself
Playing the Victim
Doubt
Insecure
A lack of confidence
Arrogance
Being traditional
Not having wisdom
Unfriendliness

WHAT YOU MAY THINK

- I am not a people person
- I don't have time to help others
- What is in it for me?
- I am shy
- It doesn't come natural
- People will begin to run over me if I do it
- What will others think of me?
- Some people take advantage of others
- I am not happy with my home
- It's mine
- I work too hard to lose it
- I am not comfortable with how my house looks
- I am selfish and don't want to share
- I don't have enough for myself let alone for other people

WAYS TO CREATE A RIPPLE

- Take off work not for personal reasons but to do something for a friend or family member.
- Instead of making just enough dinner for your family, make extra and share it with a neighbor, co-worker or extended family member.
- Busy business parents: Take the night off to take your child/children to the movies, the park or out to eat. **No cell phones!**
- Host a monthly party at home and invite your church members and/or co-workers. Create ice-breaker games and open up so that you can learn about the needs, struggles and gifts of others that you are around.
- Regardless of what is going on in your life, celebrate the success of the people around you. Encouragement is what the world is lacking.

As you provide hospitality make sure you open your heart, hands and home to others. If it is in His will, God will make sure you have more than enough to continue to be used and give to others.

Chapter Ten

Is Hospitality for You?

AS WE APPROACH the end of this book you may want to conduct a self-evaluation and ask yourself, is hospitality for me. Well, the answer is YES... If you are reading this book, you are ready to take the necessary steps to becoming more hospitable. Hospitality is not just an industry, it is a lifestyle. As you can see in the previous chapters, your hospitality is and will always be inside you. You were born with it and honestly there is nothing you can do to get rid of it. Accept your calling and allow God to use your heart for His purpose. The majority of the time you don't even have to think about it, just do it. God has given you everything you will ever need and it starts with loving Him then loving everyone else unconditionally.

Above all, love each other deeply, because love covers over a multitude of sins. Offer hospitality to one another without grumbling. Each one should use whatever gift he (she) has received to serve other, faithfully administering God's grace in its various forms. 1 Peter 4:7-10

Wrap Up!

Over the time I spent writing this book, I got caught up in watching movies about people that had cancer or other terminal illnesses. Extremely sad, I know. In these movies "True Hospitality" was displayed. People filled with compassion, tenderly touching the hearts of many families and not caring about themselves in any way during that time. They went above and beyond the call of duty making sure those people were comfortable and didn't have to worry about a thing. Honestly that is how we should be every day.

It should not take a church member to become sick and in the hospital for you to make a visit and see about their well-being. Or for you to find out that your co-worker is grieving because as a single parent she was just laid off not knowing where the next meal is going to come from. The door should have been open long before then. You should have created an open door for that church member or that single parent long before tragedy and hardship struck. Being proactive and not reactive will not only help others with their situation but it will help you get rid of procrastination in your own life and with others you care about.

It should not take something drastic to happen in order for us to be hospitable to another.

As you can see creating a ripple by practicing hospitality is extremely powerful so don't take it lightly. It tears down strongholds that we have within ourselves, gets rid of depression and selfishness and opens us up to what God truly has for us.

I invite you to change your perspective on the way you think about hospitality. Start going out of your way for others (strangers) and begin to gradually include others in your life, putting them before your personal needs. I guarantee you will begin to see an immediate change in the way you live.

Hospitality is not just an industry, it's a lifestyle.

Statement of Faith

Lord, come into my mind and my heart. Forgive me for anything that I have said, done or thought that was outside of your character and will for my life. I believe in my heart that your son died on the cross for my sins and got up on the third day. I dedicate my life to you now and always. I surrender all that I am and give you all that I have. I want to live for you.

Acknowledgements

I would like to acknowledge my **Handsome Father, William Gregory Whitlow Sr. and my Gorgeous Mother, Brenda Kay Thornton** for birthing and raising me. Thank you, Mom for being a huge part of my life. I appreciate everything you have done for me. Now it is my turn to treat you like the Queen that you are.

My Beautiful Sister, LaTamara Denise, I love you more than you will ever know. I am so proud of all of your accomplishments and I look forward to spending more time with you and Riley.

Grandma Irma Lee Thornton, you are the best Grandma a girl could ever have. Thank you for loving me and teaching me everything there is about unconditional love.

Uncle Charles and Auntie Bernita White, you two are such an inspiration to me in every part of my life. I cherish our relationship and thank you for always being there for me.

Apostle Jamie T. & Pastor Kimberly Pleasant, I can't thank you enough for being there and standing in the gap where ever needed especially spiritually. You are my spiritual parents and I love you dearly. Thanks for allowing me to grow. Pastor Kimberly, thank you being the perfect example of a Godly woman, wife and a mother. I am humbled every time I am in your presence. You are such an amazing woman of God. I pray that God continues to use you beyond your imagination and hour highest thoughts.

Erick and La'Teesha Davis, words will never be able to express the love I have for you two. When lots of people said no, you were always quick to say yes. Thank you for believing in me and supporting me throughout our friendship. True friends are extremely hard to find so I praise God I didn't have to look for you. I am really glad that God allowed out paths to cross. It is a pleasure and an honor to call you my friends.

Anita Bennett, you are such an awesome Bestie. I just want to thank you for being you and allowing me to be who God created me to be. Thanks for all of your support over the last decade. I love you more than words could ever express.

My New Zion Christian Church Family: Pastor Timothy and Tracey Brown, Pastor Quest and Teresa McKinney, Elder Lyndon and Michelle Earley, Jessica Burrell, Elder Faye Balloon, Jeremiah and Kimberly Chapman, Eric and Kre Stirgus, Kevin and Kevin and Rhonda Gardenhire, Michael and Kia Mitchell, Benjamin and Donna Jackson, Allen and Nicole Walker and the rest of my church family.

Thank you Ms. Linda for extending hospitality and allowing me to stay in your beautiful home for the nine months I didn't have anywhere else to go. Thanks for believing in and trusting me. I praise God for you. You are amazing and I pray that God continues to supply all your needs and gives you everything you want.

Ainsworth Grandison, Thank you for being my vacation as well as keeping me focused every time I thought of something else to invent, create or another company to start during my writing journey. I appreciate the walks and come to Jesus meeting you suggested I have to get me back to my goals. You inspire me to no end and I love you inside and out with my whole heart. You've helped me to walk in the true definition of hospitality.

Thank you Jamaal Hudson for the weekly Monday conference and motivation calls to make sure we both stayed on point as we wrote. I've always looked forward to those days and I appreciate the growth it created in both of us. You are such a true brother.

Thank you Sean Polidore for always holding me to a higher standard. Over the years, you have inspired me by continuing to watch and pay close attention to everything I do. I praise God for our introduction and the friendship of you and your beautiful wife.

My Diamond family: O'Keana, Alicia, Amanda Panda, Danielle Nally, Tashbina, Krista, Julian, Debbie, Meghan, Danielle Cofield, Lia, Alex, thanks for all of your support and love.

To my mentor, Pricilla Shier, I pray that one day God will allow me to travel and walk with you on the same stage teaching women across the world about the word of God. I love listening to your stories and testimonies about your family and your growth with Christ. You inspire me and I thank God for allowing you to become the woman of God that inspires many.

I would also give special thanks to a few other people:

Yolanda Sutton, Andrea Higgins, Suresh May, Rachel Lawson, Robin Ranson, Rebekah Dawn, Nikita Dawn, Carmen Mellix, Jeremiah Roberts, Sherry Saylam, Rachel Lawson, Angela Mullins Woodruff, Courtney Culmer, Nu Epps, Monica Dickerson, Diane Smith, Denise Renee', Paula Foster, Latrese Young, LaCarter and Brittany Washington, Carlos Davis, Derrick Corley and the entire Whitlow Family

AFFILIATES

Life Coaching Firm
Elite Life Coaching Through Love
www.EliteLifeCoachingThroughLove.com

LaToya Sharee
Hospitality Extraordinaire
www.LaToyaSharee.com

New Zion Christian Church
3145 Old Atlanta Road
Suwanee, GA 30024
www.NewZionChristianChurch.org

Resources

The Holy Bible was my greatest resource for this book. (New International Version 1984) – Hospitality is mentioned in the New Testament 8 times as seen below. So does that mean that they didn't show hospitality in the Old Testament? No, there are lots of scriptures that talk about how the great prophets, kings, and strangers received hospitality as they traveled.

Acts 28:7 – There was an estate nearby that belonged to Publius, the chief official of the island. He welcomed us to his home and for three days entertained us hospitably.

Romans 12:13 – Share with God's people who are in need. Practice hospitality.

Romans 16:23 – Gaius, whose hospitality I and the whole church here enjoy, sends you his greetings. Erastus, who is the city's director of public works, and our brother Quartus sends you their greetings.

1 Timothy 3:2 – Now the overseer must be above reproach, the husband of but one wife, temperate, self-controlled, respectable, hospitable, able to teach,

1 Timothy 5:10 – and is well known for her good deeds, such as bringing up children, showing hospitality, washing the feet of the saints, helping those in

trouble and devoting herself to all kinds of good deeds.

Titus 1:8 – Rather he must be hospitable, one who loves what is good, who is self-controlled, upright, holy and disciplined.

1 Peter 4:9 – Offer hospitality to one another without grumbling.

3 John 1:8 – We ought therefore to show hospitality to such men so that we may work together for the truth.

Webster, Noah. *An American Dictionary of the English Language: Intended to Exhibit…* New York: S. Converse, 1828. Print.

Open Your Heart, Open Your Hands, Open Your Home

www.ingramcontent.com/pod-product-compliance
Lightning Source LLC
Chambersburg PA
CBHW030224170426
43194CB00007BA/851